故園畫憶

庚寅中秋
韓磬逸題

《故园画忆系列》编委会

名誉主任：韩启德

主　　任：邵　鸿

委　　员：(按姓氏笔画为序)

万　捷	王秋桂	方李莉	叶培贵
刘魁立	况　晗	严绍璗	吴为山
范贻光	范　芳	孟　白	邵　鸿
岳庆平	郑培凯	唐晓峰	曹兵武

目　录

序　　　　　　　　　　　　李福顺
自序　　　　　　　　　　　王巧璞

青岛市

湛山寺	3
青岛天主教堂	4
圣保罗教堂	5
总督官邸	6
胶澳监狱	7
德国胶澳警察署旧址	8
德国海军第二营部大楼旧址	9
帝国法院旧址	10
汇丰银行青岛分行	11
麦加利银行青岛分行旧址	12
日本大连汽船株式会社	13
青岛支店旧址	13
青岛海洋大学旧址	14
圣功女子中学旧址	15
青岛市美术馆	16
青岛啤酒博物馆	17
青岛邮电博物馆	18
青岛德国监狱旧址博物馆	19
青岛市大礼堂旧址	20
老舍故居	21
安治泰公寓	22
胶州旅馆旧址	23
青岛车站旅馆旧址	24
水师饭店旧址	25
黄县路民居	26
鲁迅公园	27
栈　桥	28
海水提用泵房	29
团岛灯塔	30
小青岛	31
八大关	32
信号山	33
青岛水族馆	34
里　院	35
青岛火车站	36
花石楼	37
公主楼	38

烟台市

烟台大庙	41
阳主庙	42
烟台天主教堂	43
烟台圣会堂	44
烟台美国领事馆	45
丹麦领事馆旧址	46
烟台蚕丝专修学校旧址	47
崇正中学旧址	48
烟台第一中学	49
烟台丁氏故宅	50
南门里东巷民居	51
牟氏庄园	52
烟台街景	53
烟台火车站	54
大钟楼	55
烟台栈桥	56
张裕葡萄酒厂	57
烟台福建会馆	58
烟台东炮台表海风雄城门	59
烟台芝罘岛	60
芝罘俱乐部	61
蓬莱田横山	62
蓬莱阁	63
戚继光牌坊	64
烟台山	65
烟台山灯塔	66
烟台山老街	67
烟台山朝阳街区	68
寒同山神仙洞	69
长岛仙境阁	70
长岛九丈崖	71
毓璜顶庙会	72
烟台面塑	73

威海市

威海天后宫	77
刘公庙	78
石岛赤山大佛	79
威海宽仁院	80
海军提督署	81
水师学堂	82
中国甲午战争博物馆陈列馆	83
小红楼	84
威海四眼楼	85
海草房	86
六角楼	87
华勇营旧址	88
威海老洋房	89
威海卫	90
威海炮台	91
威海定远舰	92

幸福门	93
悦海灯塔	94
刘公岛皂埠嘴炮台	95
日岛炮台	96
海驴岛灯塔	97
成山头	98
成山头灯塔	99
圣经山	100
胶东大鼓	101
祭祀渔神	102
新船点睛	103
荣成国际渔民节	104
乳山大秧歌	105
乳山夏西火龙秧歌	106
祭海神	107

日照市	109
护国万寿光明寺（一）	111
护国万寿光明寺（二）	112
五莲山景区	113
五莲山	114
日照市街景（一）	115
日照市街景（二）	116
日照火车站	117
日照港	118
日照灯塔	119
万平口风景区	120
日照帆船基地	121
龙王节	122
渔民节（一）	123
渔民节（二）	124

Contents

Forward   Li Fushun

Preface   Qiaopu Wang

Qingdao City

Zhanshan Temple	3
Qingdao Cathedral	4
St Paul's Cathedral	5
Governor's Mansion	6
Jiao'ao Prison	7
German Jiao'ao Police DepartmentSite	8
The Site of 2nd Battlion Building of German	9
The Imperial Court Site	10
QingdaoBranch of HSBC Bank	11
Standard Chartered Bank Site	12
Site of Qingdao Branch of Japanese Dalian Steamship Co., LTD	13
Qingdao Ocean University Site	14
Site of Sheng-gong Girl's High School	15
QingdaoArt Museum	16
The Qingdao Beer Museum	17
Museum of Posts and Telecommunication of Qingdao	18
Qingdao GermanPrison Museum Site	19
Qingdao AuditoriumSite	20
Former Residence of Lao She	21
AnzerApartment	22
Jiaozhou Hotel Site	23
Site of QingdaoRailway Station Hotels	24
Navy Hotel Site	25
Local Style Dwelling Houses of Huangxian Road	26
Lu Xun Park	27
ZhanqiaoPier	28
Seawater PumpingRoom	29
Lighthouse of Tuandao Island	30
SmallQingdao Island	31
Ba Da Guan(Eight Great Streets)	32
Signal Hill	33
Qingdao Aquarium	34
Li Yuan(special Qingdao style compound)	35
QingdaoRailway Station	36
Huashi Mansion	37
The Princess Mansion	38

Yantai City

Yantai Grand Temple	41
YangzhuTemple	42

Yantai Cathedral	43	Old Street on Yantai Hill	67
Yantai Christian Church	44	Chaoyang Street on Yantai Hill	68
U.S. Consulate in Yantai	45	Fairy Cave of Hantong Hill	69
Danish Consulate Site	46	Fairyland Pavilion of Long Island	70
Yantai Silk School Site	47	Jiuzhang Cliff	71
Chongzheng Middle School Site	48	Yuhuangding Temple Fair	72
Yantai No.1 Middle School	49	Yantai Dough Sculpture	73
Ding's Former Residence	50		
Dwellings in East Lane of South Gate	51	**Weihai City**	
Mou's Manor	52	Temple of Queen of Heaven	77
Characteristics of Yantai Streets	53	Liugong Temple	78
Yantai Railway Station	54	Chishan Buddha of Stone Island	79
The Grand Clock Tower	55	Tolerance and Mercy Monastery	80
Yantai Pier	56	Navy Praefect Bureau	81
Changyu Winery	57	Naval Academy	82
Fujian Guild Hall	58	The Museum of Sino-Japanese War of 1894-1895	83
Gate of East Battery in Yantai	59	Little Red Tower	84
Yantai Zhifu Island	60	Four Eyes Building	85
Zhifu Club	61	Seaweed House	86
Penglai Tianheng Hill	62	Hexagonal Tower	87
Penglai Pavilion	63	Chinese Regiment Site	88
Memorial Arch of Qi Jiguang	64	Old Western Style Houses in Weihai	89
Yantai Hill	65	Weihai Port	90
Lighthouse on Yantai Hill	66	Weihai Forts	91

Dingyuan Warship of Weihai	92	Rizhao City	
Well BeingGate	93	The Brightness Temple of Longevity (1)	111
Yuehai Lighthouse	94	The Brightness Temple of Longevity (2)	112
Zaobuzhui Fort in Liugong in Island	95	Five LotusMountain Scenic Area	113
Sun Island Fort	96	Five Lotus Mountain	114
Lighthouse of Hailu Island	97	Street View of Rizhao City (1)	115
Cheng Hilltop	98	Street View of Rizhao City (2)	116
Lighthouse on Cheng Hilltop	99	Rizhao Railway Station	117
Bible Hill	100	Rizhao Port	118
Jiaodong Bass Drum	101	Rizhao Lighthouse	119
To Worship the God ofFishing	102	WanpingkouScenic Area	120
Putting in the Pupils on a New Boat	103	Sailing Boat Base of Rizhao	121
Rongcheng International Fishermen Festival	104	The Dragon King Festival	122
Rushan Dayangge	105	Fishermen Festival (1)	123
Rushan Xiaxi Huolong Yangge	106	Fishermen Festival (2)	124
To Worship the God of Sea	107		

序

  第一次见巧璞是在他高一新学期的画室里，他是个个子高高但满脸稚气的大眼睛男生。和其他同学不同的是，每次上完专业课，他都会留下和我聊聊画、聊聊天。这一聊，就一直聊到了现在。

  一有回忆，就有感慨，唏嘘时光荏苒、岁月沉浮。这么多年，从男孩到男人，从王同学到王老师，巧璞那颗向往自由的心在经历了生活的逆流顺流之后，被洗刷得可以以一种更包容的态度去对待这个复杂的世界，也更加能够从中活得快乐。而对于专业、对于绘画，巧璞却整个人都变得柔软起来，温柔地去呵护生命中那些重要的组成部分。生活是一种态度，绘画是一种生活，如何用绘画表现生活，如何用绘画表达一种态度，是每一位美术工作者面临的和需要思考的问题。

  关于这些画，是用最简单材料、最直接的绘画方式，呈现出来的那些我们熟悉的建筑。从中我们可以看到造型与结构，可以感受到岁月的沉淀，可以体验到绘画性的视觉愉悦感。同时，这些画还表达了一种态度，一种对待生活的态度、一种对待绘画的态度。

  我们还能要求些什么呢？

李福顺
2015年3月

Forward

I met Qiaopu for the first time at the art studio when he was a freshman in high school. He was a tall boy with a childlike face. Every time after class, he would stay with me for a while, chatting and talking about paintings. Since then, we have kept in touch

Time flies with the years rolling on. From a boy to a man, from a student to a teacher, the heart of Qiaopu, which yearned for freedom, became more tolerant by the washing of life. Through his painting, Qiaopu became completely soft and took good care of his craft as the most importantpart of his life. Painting is a kind of attitude as well as akind of life. Howto use painting to express life and attitudeis the issue everyartist will face.

In regard to the sketches in this book, Qiaopu used the simplest materials and most direct expressions to show us the familiar architecture. We can see the modeling and structure while feelingthe precipitation of time and enjoying the visual pleasure from these sketches. At the same time, these sketches also express a kind of attitude towards life and the painting.

What else can we ask for?

Li Fushun
March, 2015

Preface

I have always wished to get out of the city and approach the earth in a field in the countryside-primitive simplicity, architecture and folk customs. The sense of reality and culture in perfect harmony makes me feel that our existence is inseparable with culture as we can only have a root and a home to return to with culture.

Thanks to the Academy Press for giving me the honor to participate in the "Memory of Old Homes in Sketches" project. This gives me an opportunity to express my inner fascination with culture and interpret the beauty of ancient buildings and folk-customs with my own perspective.

I hope this book can be a proper elaboration and expression of ancient culture. The sketch is a kind of natural and friendly language. You can touch the deep nature of the art spirit from the transformation of lines. In this book, I intuitively experienced the historical process of cultural evolution while expressing the desire to experience culture; culture is the flame that burns our hearts and guides our way forward. Only culture can make the meaning of our existence deeper. It seems that my wish to sketch culture is becoming possible by catching the mind's view with artistic language.

This book of The Sketches of East Shandong mainly collects drawings of ancient architecture, customs and the culture of east Shandong. I conducted a complete carding on the history, culture and folk-customs of Shandong on the premise of respecting the original appearance of ancient buildings and folk-customs while sketching the outline of the culture in Southwestern Shandong to reproduce its historical and cultural characteristics.

Due to the immature nature of my artistic language, the limits of my sketching level and the short time I had to create, error is inevitable. Corrections and comments from the readers are appreciated.

Qiaopu Wang
2016

青岛市

湛山寺

　　位于青岛市市南区芝泉路二号，建于1934年。从山门到藏经楼共四进，分中、西、东三个院落；山门有横匾金字"湛山寺"。湛山寺前的放生池是蓄山泉之水而成，池畔有兰亭，白玉观音菩萨立于池中；山门前一对石狮肃立法门，石狮雕琢精细。为市区唯一的佛寺。

Zhanshan Temple

Located at No. 2, Zhiquan Road, ShinanDistrict, it was built in 1934. There are four rows of buildings from the gate to the scripture-storage tower and the temple consists of three yards: Middle, West and East.It is the onlyBuddhist temple in the downtown area.

青岛天主教堂

　　原称"圣弥厄尔教堂",位于青岛市市南区浙江路15号。始建于1932年,占地面积约1.15万平方米;由德国设计师毕娄哈依据哥德式和罗马式建筑风格设计而成。平面呈"十"字形,大门上方有一巨大的玫瑰窗,两侧各耸立一座56米高的钟塔,塔尖各有一高4.5米的十字架。此为中国唯一的祝圣教堂。

Qingdao Cathedral

Originally known as St. Michael's Cathedral,located at No.15, Zhejiang Road, Shinan District, it was built in 1932 and designed by German architect Bialucha in the gothic and Roman styles It is the only consecrated church in China.

圣保罗教堂

又名"观象二路基督教堂"，位于青岛市市南区观象二路一号的高地上。始建于1938年，由俄国建筑师尤力甫设计的仿罗马风格的基督教堂。红清水砖墙，标志性的钟楼高24米，是青岛五大钟楼之一。

St Paul's Cathedral

Also known as the Christian Church of Second Guanxiang Road, located on the highlands of No. 1, Second Guanxiang Road, Shinan District, it was built in 1938 and designed by Russian architect Yourieff in the Romanesque style. The bell tower is 24 meters tall and is regarded as one of the top fivetowers in Qingdao.

总督官邸

　　俗称"提督府",位于青岛市市南区龙山路26号,始建于清光绪三十一年(1905年)。由德国建筑师拉查鲁维茨设计,是当时占领青岛的德国提督官邸,故名总督官邸。建筑面积4083平方米,是典型的德国威廉时代的德式建筑。

Governor's Mansion

Commonly known as Praefect Mansion, located at No. 26, Longshan Road, Shinan District, it was built in 1905 and designed by German architect, Lazarowicz. It is typical of German architecture from William's time.

胶澳监狱

又名"欧人监狱"，位于青岛市市南区常州路23号，建成于清光绪二十六年（1900年）。该建筑群以两层德国古堡式建筑为主体，包括伙房、浴室、监房、瞭望台等。与主体建筑镶嵌在一起的塔楼，其墙面上有依内部的47级螺旋楼梯设置的条形窗口，站在塔楼顶部可以观察监狱外部动向。

Jiao'ao Prison

Also known as"European Prison", located at No. 23, Changzhou Road, ShinanDistrict, it was completed in 1900 as an important modern building in Qingdao.The main body is a two-storey building modeled after a German castle with a connecting tower. Standing on top of the tower, the situation outside the prison can be observed.

德国胶澳警察署旧址

位于青岛市市南区湖北路29号，建于清光绪三十年（1904年），现为青岛市公安局。其造型取中世纪以来德国村镇教堂型制，显示浓重的西欧城市街景的格调，为德国文艺复兴式建筑风格和欧陆中世纪教堂建筑风格。

German Jiao'ao Police DepartmentSite

Located at No.29, Hubei Road, Shinan District, built in 1904, today it is the Qingdao Municipal Public Security Bureau. It combines the styles of German Renaissance architecture and a European medieval church.

德国海军第二营部大楼旧址

　　位于青岛市市南区沂水路9号,建于清光绪二十五年(1899年),属青岛年代最久的建筑之一。建筑面积1515平方米,德国文艺复兴式建筑风格。

The Site of 2nd Battlion Building of German
NavyLocated at No. 9, Yishui Road, Shinan District, it was built in 1899 and is one of the oldest buildings in Qingdao with a construction area of 1,515 square meters. It is in the German Renaissance architectural style.

帝国法院旧址

　　位于青岛市市南区德县路2号，始建于1912年。始为胶州帝国法院办公楼，后为青岛历届法院驻地，今为市南区检察院。两层砖石木结构，红瓦蒙莎屋顶，黄色拉毛墙面附浅壁柱，蘑菇石勒脚，具有德国建筑厚重粗犷的特点。

The Imperial Court Site

Located at No. 2, Dexian Road, Shinan District, it was built in 1912 withGermanarchitectural characteristics, solid and rough. It was the office building of the Jiaozhou Imperial Court before becoming the site of the Qiaodao Court. Now, it is the site of the procuratorate of Shinan District.

汇丰银行青岛分行

位于青岛市市北区馆陶路5号，竣工于1917年。建筑面积3150平方米，德式风格建筑。立面以十字路口中心向两侧自然展开；一、二层的表面弧度十分圆润自然，各有一座山墙，风格各异，但都在正上方开老虎窗；三层为阁楼层，罩孟莎式屋顶。

QingdaoBranch of HSBC Bank

Located at No. 5, Guantao Road at Wusong road, Shibei District, the German style building was completed in 1917 covering an area of 3,150 square meters. The vertical side of the building was spread naturally to both sides, with the intersection as the center.There is an attic on the third floor.

麦加利银行青岛分行旧址

位于青岛市市北区馆陶路2号。麦加利银行青岛分行于1925年设立，有资本金300万英镑。建筑风格混合了演变中的欧洲建筑语言，入口和窗口的装饰比较简化，斜坡屋顶的处理又明显具有东方意味。

Standard Chartered Bank Site

Located at No.2, Guantao Road, Shibei District, the Qingdao Branch of Standard Chartered Bank was established in 1925. The architectureblends with transitional European styles and the slopingroof is obvious Oriental style.

日本大连汽船株式会社青岛支店旧址

　　位于青岛市市北区馆陶路37号,始建于1927年,欧式风格。整栋建筑造型刻意建成船形,大楼沿两街交口处展开立面,三段式构图,基座采用粗糙的石块砌筑,以两个巨大的石柱支撑,檐口下方刻有石雕花饰。

Site of Qingdao Branch of Japanese Dalian Steamship Co., LTD

Located at No. 37, Guantao Road, Shibei district, it is an European style building built in 1927. The whole building was deliberately modeled into the shape of a ship with a stone base supported by huge stone columns. There are ornatestone carvings under the eaves.

青岛海洋大学旧址

位于青岛市市南区鱼山路5号,今为中国海洋大学鱼山校区,始建于1924年。1958年以前这里是青岛大学的所在地,更早前则是德国俾斯麦兵营,受此因素的影响,校园至今还保留着德国建筑的风貌。许多著名的作家,如老舍、梁实秋、沈从文、闻一多、吴伯箫、洪深等都曾在此执教。

Qingdao Ocean University Site

Located in the Yushan campus of Ocean University of China, and it was built in 1924. It was the site of Qingdao University before 1958 and the barracks of Bismarck earlier. Hence the campus still keepsits German architectural style.

圣功女子中学旧址

位于青岛市市南区德县路27号，1931年美国天主教圣方济会开办女子中学，定名为"青岛私立圣功女子中学"。办学主旨是扩大天主教的影响，同时宣扬美国的生活方式。1952年改名为"山东省青岛第七中学"。

Site of Sheng-gong Girl's High School

Located at No. 27, Dexian Road, Shinan District, it was set up by American Franciscan in 1931. The original name was QingdaoPrivate Sheng-gong Girl's High Schooland it was renamed to Shandong Qingdao No. 7 Middle School in 1952.

青岛市美术馆

位于青岛市市南区大学路7号，始建于1934年，原为"万字会"旧址，现为青岛市美术馆。三进两院、五教合一的建筑。将罗马柱廊式、中国宫殿式、阿拉伯式三种不同的建筑风格集中在一起。

QingdaoArt Museum

Located at No. 7, Daxue Road, Shinan District,it was built in 1934 as the site of Wan Zihui, which was a charity organization, and it is the site of the Qingdao Art Museum now.It'sarchitecture combinesfive religious styles and consists of three rows of buildings and two yards.

| 青岛啤酒博物馆 |

位于青岛市市北区登州路56号的青岛啤酒厂老厂房内,建于清光绪二十九年(1903年)。一幢幢红色的洋房很有味道,靠马路的房子屋顶上,装饰着一排排超大啤酒罐,格外醒目。在博物馆内,你可以了解到青岛啤酒的历史,看生产啤酒的老设备,还可以品尝到纯正的青岛啤酒。

The Qingdao Beer Museum
Located in the former workshop of the Qingdao Beer Factory at No. 56, Dengzhou Road,Shibei District, it was built in 1903.In the museum, you can learn about the history of Qingdao beer while looking at the old equipment andtasting the authentic Qingdao brew.

> 青岛邮电博物馆

　　位于青岛市市南区安徽路5号，建于清光绪二十七年（1901年），原为胶澳德意志帝国邮局。这座哥特式建筑傍栈桥、枕涛声，静立于前海；红砖清水墙外立面、半环外廊、尖顶双子塔楼，具有老派雅致的欧洲气质。

Museum of Posts and Telecommunication of Qingdao
Located at No. 5, Anhui Road, Shinan District, it was built in 1901 as Jiao'ao German Imperial Post Office. Itsarchitecture is Gothic with an elegant European style.

青岛德国监狱旧址博物馆

位于青岛市市南区常州路23号,建于清光绪二十六年(1900年)。建筑由"仁、义、礼、智、信"五座监房和一座工厂组成,"仁"字监房即青岛德式监狱旧址,其余建筑为20世纪二三十年代所建。青岛德国监狱是全国现存最早的殖民监狱旧址之一。

Qingdao GermanPrison Museum Site

Located at No. 23, Changzhou Road, ShinanDistricts, built in 1900, it consists of fiveprison houses named Ren, Yi, Li, Zhi, Xin and one workshop. It is one of theearliest colonial prison sites remaining.

青岛市大礼堂旧址

　　位于青岛市市南区兰山路1号，南与栈桥隔街相望，西邻中山路。始建于1934年，建筑面积1500多平方米。20世纪三四十年代这里一直是青岛召开大型会议和开展文艺活动的重要场所，现为青岛音乐厅。

Qingdao AuditoriumSite

Located at No. 1, Lanshan Road, Shinan District, it was built in 1934, and it is amodern European-style buildingwith aconstruction area of 1,500 square meters. It was an important venue for conferences and cultural activities in Qingdao. It is now the Qingdao Concert Hall.

老舍故居

　　又名"骆驼祥子博物馆",位于青岛市市南区黄县路12号。面南背北,楼下曾为老舍全家居所。老舍于1934年来青岛受聘于山东大学,直至1937年离开青岛,大部分时间居住于此。这是他在青岛的三处借寓住所之一,另两处一处在莱芜路,一处在金口路。

Former Residence of Lao She

Also known as Rickshaw Boy Museum, it is located at No.12, Huangxian Road, Shinan District. Employed by Shandong University, Lao She came to Qingdao in 1934 and lived in this house until he left in 1937. This is one of his three residences in Qingdao.

安治泰公寓

又名"青岛天主教会公寓",位于青岛市市南区江苏路和湖南路交叉口的西南角,建成于清光绪二十五年(1899年)。安治泰是天主教圣言会在中国,尤其是山东的重要传教士,任山东南境代牧区的代理主教。

AnzerApartment

Also known as Qingdao Catholic Church Appartment, located at the southwest corner of the intersection of Jiangsu Road and Hunan Road, Shinan District, it was completed in 1899. Anzer was an important missionary of the Catholic Divine Word Missionarie in ShandongChina.

胶州旅馆旧址

位于青岛市市南区中山路17号，建于清光绪三十四年（1908年），造型以德国古典复兴样式为主，又融合了折中主义风格。总面积1800平方米，清水红砖砌墙，三层，临街建有三米高的红砖圆券式大窗。

Jiaozhou Hotel Site

Located at No.17, Zhongshan Road, Shinan District, built in 1908, it is three-storey building with a total area of 1,800 square meters. It has a delicate architectural appearance and German classical revival style of modeling combines with the eclectic style.

<u>青岛车站旅馆旧址</u>

  又名"站前旅馆",位于青岛市市南区兰山路28号,建于1913年,由德国人R.玛特维希设计。高两层,上有阁楼和老虎窗,外墙有装饰性的山花,山墙式样为新巴洛克式。主入口设在拐角处,其上是八角形塔楼,上置逐节收缩的尖顶,与车站广场对面的车站钟楼形成了完美的对景。

Site of QingdaoRailway Station Hotels
Also known as Zhanqian Hotel, located at No. 28, Lanshan Road, Shinan District, it was built in 1913 and designed by the German, R. Matt Vichy. It is a two-storey building with a main entrance in the corner and an octagonal tower on top of the entrance.

水师饭店旧址

又名"德国海军俱乐部",位于青岛市市南区湖北路17号,始建于清光绪二十七年(1901年)。为德国新文艺复兴风格三段式建筑,是青岛早期德国建筑的代表作之一。地上三层,带阁楼,地下一层;一层有东西向礼堂,面积约300平方米,高约15米,穹顶天花板,采用非对称布局。

Navy Hotel Site

Also known as German Navy Club, it is located at No. 17, Hubei Road, Shinan District and built in 1901. It consists of three storeys on the ground and one storey underground. It is new German Renaissance architectural style and one of the representative works of early German architecture in Qingdao.

黄县路民居

位于青岛市市南区，是典型的青岛式老街，红瓦老楼，树影斑驳，以它独有的地理丰姿而蜚声海内。民国时期许多名士文人不谋而合地在这条静谧的老街上居住。

Local Style Dwelling Houses of Huangxian Road

It is located at Huangxian Road, ShinanDistrict, adjacent to the former Shandong University, museum, library and hotel.Many celebrities and scholars chose to live here coincidentallyduring the period of the Republic of China.

鲁迅公园

位于青岛市市南区莱阳路南侧，建于1929年，著名园艺家葛敬应先生借其抱岸环海的自然环境依势而造，1950年为纪念鲁迅先生而易名。公园大门前眉刻有"鲁迅公园"四个金字，集鲁迅手迹而成，为青岛最具特色的临海公园。

Lu Xun Park

Located at the south of Laiyang Road, ShinanDistrict, it was built based on its natural location in 1929 byhorticulturist Mr. GeJingying.In 1950, it was renamed Lu Xun Park to commemorate Mr. Lu Xun. Itis the most unique coastal park in Qingdao.

| 栈 桥 |

位于青岛市市南区太平路12号,始建于清光绪十八年(1892年),已有百年历史,是青岛最早的军事专用人工码头。栈桥素有"长虹远引"之美誉,被视为青岛市的重要标志。栈桥的尽头建有三角形防波堤和一座具有民族风格的八角亭阁"回澜阁"。

ZhanqiaoPier

Located at No. 12, Taiping Road, ShinanDistrict, it was build in 1892 and has a history of over one hundred years.It was the earliest special military artificial pier in Qingdao. Zhanqiao Pier has always been known as "Rainbow Stretching to the Sea" and is regarded as an important symbol of Qingdao.

海水提用泵房

位于青岛市市南区栈桥外,门牌号"太平路12号",建于清光绪二十八年(1902年),为抽水用泵站,由德国人建造,目的是抽海水以泼洒路面用。

Seawater PumpingRoom

Located at No. 12, Taiping Road, next to a public toilet outside of Zhanqiao Pier, it was built by Germans in 1902 as a water pumping room to draw seawater to splash on the pavement.

团岛灯塔

曾名"游内山灯塔",位于青岛市市南区,建于清光绪二十六年(1900年),建筑总高15.4米。第一次世界大战期间,灯塔及各种设施遭到破坏,日本占领青岛后,修复了各种设施,并保留了灯塔和机房等德式建筑。灯塔为八角形石砌结构,内有螺旋形楼梯直通塔顶,灯塔上还装有一种特殊的导航设备——气雾号。

Lighthouse of Tuandao Island

Formerly known as the Lighthouse of Younei Mountain, located in Shinan District, it was built in 1900 with a total height of 15.4 meters. It is an octagonal stone structure with an internal spiral staircase that leads to the top. A special audio navigation equipment called the steam horn was installed on top of the lighthouse.

> 小青岛

又名"琴岛",位于青岛市市南区琴屿路2号,原先是陆地的一部分,因长期受海水的侵蚀,渐与陆地分离,形成了今天的形状,像一把古琴,所以又叫"琴岛"。青岛城市的名称就来源于小青岛。

SmallQingdao Island

Also known as Qin (which means musical instrument)Island, located atNo. 2, Qinyu Road, Shinan District, it was originally part of the land and gradually separated and formed the shape it has today because of longterm sea water erosion.

[八大关]

　　位于青岛市市南区黄海路，"八大关"起初是指以我国著名关隘命名的八条道路（韶关路、宁武关路、紫荆关路、武胜关路、嘉峪关路、正阳关路、居庸关路、山海关路），后来成为泛指。八大关现有300多座别墅，多为20世纪初中外政客富商所建，现今成了单位疗养院和政府机构驻地。

Ba Da Guan(Eight Great Streets)

Located at Huanghai Road,ShinanDistrict, Ba Da Guan consists of more than 300 villas, most of which were built by Chinese and foreign politicians and merchants in the early 20th century.Now it is the site of nursing homesand government offices.

信号山

　　又名"挂旗山",位于青岛市市南区龙山路16号。海拔98米,前临大海,背依市区,是观赏海景和市区风貌的最佳观景点之一。青岛港建成后,山上建有信旗台,专为轮船及帆船入港时传递信号,故得名"信号山"。

Signal Hill

Also known as Flag Hill, located at No. 16, Longshan Road, Shinan District, this 98-meter-high hill is one of the best observation places to enjoy seaview and city sights with its unique location.

青岛水族馆

　　位于青岛市市南区莱阳路2号，建于1930年，高四层，建于海滩岩石之上。该建筑为重檐歇山屋顶宫殿式建筑，在当时青岛纷纷采用欧式建筑的情况下，唯独青岛水族馆选择了中国城垣式古典民族建筑造型，是中国也是亚洲的第一座水族馆。

Qingdao Aquarium

Located at No. 2, Laiyang Road, ShinanDistrict, this four-storey building was built on the rocks in the beach in 1930. This multiple eave hippedroof architecture is the firstaquarium in China and Asia.

里 院

　　位于青岛市市南区保定路,建于20世纪初,里院为方形,四周围合,中心形成一个大院;两到三层,底层多为商业用途,二层以上为住宅。从平面布局来看,是一种比较典型的西方近代规划模式,但是每一个街坊中的院落及其内部构成却兼具中式建筑的特点,是中西折中式建筑。

Li Yuan(special Qingdao style compound)

Located at Baoding Road, ShinanDistrict, built in the early 20th century, Li Yuan is a typical square compound with a big yard in the center. Most buildings inside are two-storeys and three-storeys with shops on the first floor and apartments on the second and third floors. It is a kind of special architecture combining Western and Chinese styles.

青岛火车站

位于青岛市市南区泰安路1号,始建于清光绪二十六年(1900年),为德国人魏尔勒和格德尔茨设计,是德占时期的经典建筑,建筑风格为德国文艺复兴风格。

QingdaoRailway Station

Located at No.1, Tai'an Road, ShinanDistrict, it was built in 1900 and designed by Germanarchitects Werner and Gerd Scholz. It's classic architecture is typical of the German occupation period, with a German Renaissance architectural style.

花石楼

　　位于青岛市市南区黄海路18号,建于1931年,主体共五层,顶层为观海台,外墙全部用花岗岩砌成,塔楼顶部为雉堞式女儿墙,是一幢融合了西方多种建筑艺术风格的欧洲古堡式建筑,是青岛颇具特色的著名建筑。

Huashi Mansion
Located at No.18, Huanghai Road, ShinanDistrict, it was built in 1931 as a five-storey European castle style building with a seaview platform on top.It is a famous building in Qingdao.

公主楼

位于青岛市市南区居庸关路16号,始建于20世纪30年代中期,占地近千平方米,建筑面积约722平方米,由一座尖塔与不规则斜顶屋组成,南部有方型平台,好像童话故事中的建筑。该建筑为北欧滨海风格庭院建筑。

The Princess Mansion

Located at No.16, Juyongguan Road, ShinanDistrict, built in the mid-1930's, it consists of a steeple,irregular inclined top house and square platform in the south. It is a Northern European coastal style courtyard building.

烟台市
Yantai City

烟台大庙

位于烟台市芝罘区，为龙王庙、海神庙、天后宫的三庙合一，故称为"大庙"。"大"不是指规模，而是一庙多殿或多神的意思。

Yantai Grand Temple

Located in the Zhifu District, it is a combination of the Dragon King Temple, Sea God Temple and Temple of the Queen of Heaven. Grand Temple does not signify the size but means that there is more than one god in the temple.

阳主庙

    位于烟台市芝罘区芝罘岛，始建于春秋战国时期，是齐国国君奉祀"八神将"的庙宇之一。阳主庙里立了阳主和其妻子塑像，供人进香，其他房间则有描绘鬼魂在地狱受苦的场景。

YangzhuTemple

Located onZhifu Island,Zhifu District, built during the Spring and Autumn Warring States period(770 B.C.-221 B.C.) by the Emperor of the Qi Kingdom to enshrine eight heroic generals. There are statues of Yangzhu and his wife in the templefor people to offer incense.

> 烟台天主教堂

  全称"玛利亚进教之佑圣母堂",位于烟台市芝罘区海岸街24号,始建于1868年,为意大利神甫昂智鲁斯奉罗马教庭之命创建。建筑面积3800平方米,平面为十字架型的法式哥特式尖顶教堂。

Yantai Cathedral
Located at No. 24, Coastal Street, Zhifu District, built in 1868 by an Italian priest. it is a French gothic style church and its full name is the "Church of Mary, Help of Christians."

烟台圣会堂

位于蓬莱市，始建于清同治十一年（1872年），原为美式建筑，由礼拜堂和钟楼联体构成。因年久失修，损毁严重，1987年修缮。东部礼拜堂为单层结构，神坛坐东朝西，正中设有洗礼池，两侧为更衣房，堂内可容纳近400人。西部钟楼旧为三层，顶楼木梁上悬有铜钟，每值礼拜日，钟声响彻全城。

Yantai Christian Church

Located in Penglai City, it was built in 1872 as an American style building with an eastern chapel that can accommodate nearly 400 people. The west tower is a three-storey building with a bronze bell on top of the wooden beams. Every Sunday, the bell resounds throughout the city.

烟台美国领事馆

　　位于烟台市芝罘区历山路，建于20世纪初，由烟台市德成营造厂建造。砖木混合结构的二层楼房，建筑平面呈方形，红瓦覆顶，双面外连廊，四面坡屋顶，有阁楼窗，中间为玻璃顶，下接二层室内吹拨共享厅，室内木装修多为曲线式装饰。

U.S.Consulate in Yantai
Located at Lishan Road, Zhifu District,it was built by Yantai Decheng Construction Firm in the early 20th century. It is a 2-storey, wooden, square structure with a masonry Most of the internal wooden decorations are curved

丹麦领事馆旧址

位于烟台市芝罘区烟台山西路,建于清同治六年(1867年),建筑采用近代建筑设计手法,砖混结构。

Danish Consulate Site

Located at Yantaishan West Road, Zhifu District, and built in 1867, it is a brick-concrete structure which adopted modern architectural design.

烟台蚕丝专修学校旧址

位于烟台市芝罘区南山路1号,建于清光绪三十年(1904年),由法国天主教神父设计。主体建筑为砖混结构二层楼房,建筑面积700平方米,建筑平面近似方形,对角线两端(东南与西北)各矗立三层方尖顶角楼,现为桑蚕原种厂。

Yantai Silk School Site

Located at No.1, Nanshan Road, Zhifu District, it was built in 1904 and designed by a French Catholic priest. The main building is a 2-storey brick-concrete structure with a construction area of 700 square meters. It is a silkworm plant now.

崇正中学旧址

　　位于烟台市芝罘区大马路东段，始建于1931年，由法国天主教方济会神父设计，带有法国早期古典主义风格。每栋楼对角线的两端为三层角楼，其他部分皆为两层，红铁皮四面坡屋顶，青砖砌墙，清水边柜，使用西方古典式样的青砖雕和木雕，优雅素朴。

ChongzhengMiddle SchoolSite

Located at the east of Damalu Road,Zhifu Distric, designed by a French Catholic priest, it was built in 1931 with an early French classical style.

烟台第一中学

　　原名"芝罘中学",位于烟台市芝罘区东端二马路17号,始建于1931年。1950年为山东省最早的十五处重点中学之一,1993年被命名为山东省首批规范化学校。

Yantai No.1 Middle School

Formerly known as ZhifuMiddle School, located at No. 17, Ermalu Road, the east of Zhifu District, it was built in 1931.In 1950, itwas one of the earliest fifteen key middle schools in Shandong province.

【烟台丁氏故宅】

　　位于龙口市黄城西大街，建于清代中期，占地3.106万平方米，建筑面积8042平方米，是目前中国规模宏大、保存较好的"四合院"式建筑群。

Ding's Former Residence
Located in the Huangcheng West Street, Longkou City, it was built in the middle Qing Dynasty(1644-1911) with a construction area of 8,042 square meters. It is one of the largest preserved courtyard groups in China.

南门里东巷民居

　　位于烟台市芝罘区南门里东巷，建于清代末期，清咸丰十一年（1861年）烟台开埠，标志着烟台半殖民地化的开始。西方列强乘虚而入，纷纷涉足这古老的海滨。港口与港埠民族工业之间的相互促进和发展，为人们提供了较多的就业机会，很多人来此定居。

Dwellings in East Lane of South Gate

Located in the East Lane, South Gate,Zhifu District,it was built in the lateQing Dynasty(1644-1911). Opened as a commercial port in 1861, Yantai became asemi-colony and many people came here to work and settledown.

【牟氏庄园】

又称"牟二黑庄园",位于栖霞市城北古镇都村,始建于清雍正年间(1722～1735年),到1935年形成现在的规模,是牟墨林家族几代人居住的地方。庄园坐北朝南,包括六个大院,占地两万多平方米,建有万堂楼厢480多间。

Mou'sManor

Also known asMou Er Hei Manor, located in Du Village, Chengbei Town, Qixia City, it was built from 1722 to 1735 as the residence of Mou Molin's family. Mou was the biggest landlord in northern China and generations of his family lived here.

烟台街景

　　烟台地形为低山丘陵区，属于温带季风气候，依山傍海，空气温润，境内名胜古迹众多，是旅游避暑和休闲度假的胜地。

Characteristics of YantaiStreets

Yantai,one of the first 14 coastal cities opened to the outside world in China, has been awarded many times as the National Civilized Port by the National Port Office.

> 烟台火车站

　　位于烟台市芝罘区芝罘屯路，始建于1956年。设计规模为五台八线，隶属于济南铁路局管辖，现为客货运一等站。

Yantai RailwayStation
Located at Zhifutun Road,Zhifu District, it was built in 1956 with five platforms and eight lines. Now it isa first-class station for both passengersand cargo.

大钟楼

位于烟台市芝罘区南大街上，建于1982年，可以说是烟台市中心的中心。烟台是近代造钟工业的发祥地，大钟楼是烟台地标性建筑物之一。

The GrandClock Tower

Located at Nandajie Street, Zhifu District,it was built in 1982.Yantai is the birthplace of the modern clock industry and the Grand Clock Tower is one of its landmarks.

烟台栈桥

　　位于烟台市芝罘区东部，全长624米，宽10米，由引桥、游艇码头、栈桥主体、黄海明珠四部分组成，是目前我国最长的海上栈桥。

Yantai Pier

Located at the easternZhifu District, it is 624 meters long, 10 meters wide and consists of four parts named "Approaching Bridge,", "Marina,", "Pier Body," and the "Pearl of the Yellow Sea." It is the longest pier in China.

张裕葡萄酒厂

位于烟台市芝罘区大马路56号，建于清光绪十八年（1892年），南洋华侨张弼士创办，中国最早的葡萄酒厂。其建筑包括南大门、厂房、宿舍楼、地下酒窖等，木砖石结构，面积两万多平方米。

Changyu Winery

Located at No. 56, Damalu Road, Zhifu District, it covers an area of more than twenty thousand square meters and was built in 1892 by Zhang Bishi, a Chinese man living oversees. It was one of the earliest wineries in China.

烟台福建会馆

又称"天后行宫",位于烟台市芝罘区南大街与胜利路交汇处。始建于清光绪十年(1884年),是福建籍商人集会联谊的场所。会馆坐南朝北,占地3500平方米,原三进院,现存两进,皆为砖石木结构,闽南风格,时称"鲁东第一"。

Fujian Guild Hall
Also known as the Palace of the Queen of Heaven, it is located at theintersection of Nandajie Street and Shengli Road in the Zhifu District.It was built in 1884 as a gathering place for businessmen from Fujian.The north-facing building is a brick and wood structure in the Southern Fujian style. Only two houses remain.

烟台东炮台表海风雄城门

　　位于烟台市芝罘区滨海北路，建于清代末期，因景区内岿岱山上一座保存完好的清末炮台而得名，东炮台与西炮台遥相对峙，正面拱门上方有清末著名新派人物马建忠的题额"表海风雄"。

Gate of East Battery in Yantai
Located at Binhai North Road, Zhifu District, it was built in the late Qing Dynasty(1644-1911) and named after the well-preserved battery on Kuidai Hill.

烟台芝罘岛

　　位于烟台市芝罘区，芝罘岛是烟台港湾的一道天然防波堤，从整个地形看，宛若一棵灵芝草，生长在碧波万顷的黄海之中。

Yantai Zhifu Island

Located in the Zhifu District, it is a natural seawall of Yantai Harbour. From the air, it is like a glossy ganodermagrowing in the boundless expanse of the blue water of the YellowSea.

> 芝罘俱乐部

　　又名 "外国总会"，位于烟台市芝罘区海岸路西端，始建于清同治四年（1865年），东临大海，北依烟台山，系外国侨民在烟台开设的娱乐场所。初为平房数间，1913年由英籍基督教牧师卜尔耐特设计，改建成现在的三层楼房，木石结构，建筑面积3100平方米。

ZhifuClub
Also known as Foreigner's Club, located at Western Hai'an Road, Zhifu District, it was built in 1865 as an entertainment venue for foreigners livingin Yantai. The sea is to the east and Yantai Hill is to the north.

[蓬莱田横山]

又名"老北山",位于蓬莱市迎宾路59号,因公元前202年齐王田横与五百壮士的壮举,后人将此山命名为"田横山"。

Penglai Tianheng Hill

Also known as Laobei Hill, it is located at No. 59, Yingbin Road, Penglai City.In 202 B.C., Tianheng, the emperor of the Qi Kingdom, and his 500 soldiers committed suicide here instead of surrendering to the Han Emperor, Liubang. It was named after this.

蓬莱阁

位于胶东半岛最北端蓬莱市丹崖山上,始建于北宋嘉祐六年(1061年),素有"人间仙境"之称。传说蓬莱是海中神仙居住之所,亦是秦始皇东寻求药、汉武帝御驾访仙之地,蓬莱阁与黄鹤楼、岳阳楼、滕王阁并称中国四大名楼。

Penglai Pavilion

Located at the northern end of Jiaodong peninsula, known as "Fairyland on Earth," it was built in 1061 and was listed as one of the four most famous Chinese famous pavilions, together with Yellow Crane Tower, Yueyang Tower and the Pavilion of Prince Teng.

戚继光牌坊

位于蓬莱市区内戚家祠堂南门,建于明嘉靖四十四年(1565年),是明朝廷为褒扬抗倭戍边名将戚继光及其父戚景通而建。花岗岩石雕,正间上下三坊,镂雕"丹凤朝阳""二龙戏珠""狮子滚绣球"等图案,侧间各有两坊,分别雕有花木鸟兽等图案。

Memorial Arch of Qi Jiguang

Located at the south gate of Qi's ancestral temple in Penglai City, it was built by the royal court in 1565 to commend the anti-Japaneseachievements of the famous general,Qi Jiguang and his father, QiJingtong during the Ming Dynasty(1368-1644). The arch was made of granite carved with various flowers,trees, birds and animals.

烟台山

　　位于烟台市芝罘区厉新路，明洪武三十一年（1398年）在藤峰顶设立烽烟台，作为报警的场所，因而称为"烟台山"，后来烟台市也由此得名。山下至今还有明代抗倭名将戚继光驻兵饮马的营房里、马房里、马厂街等遗迹。因为烟台山地势重要，所以元朝曾在这里筑垒架炮。

Yantai Hill

It is located in Lixin Road, Zhifu District. In 1398, the royal court built BeaconTower on TengPeak and it was called Yantai Hill, which means beacon hill. Yantai City was also named after this.

烟台山灯塔

　　位于烟台市芝罘区历新路，始建于清光绪三十一年（1905年），由英国人建造，后因年久失修，20世纪80年代初被拆除，现存建于1988年，是烟台市唯一的标志性建筑。

Lighthouse on Yantai Hill

Located in Lixin Road, Zhifu District, it was built in 1905 by the British and demolished in the early 1980's due to long years of being out of repair. Rebuilt in 1988, it is the only landmarkof Yantai City.

烟台山老街

　　位于烟台市芝罘区厉新路，老街在烟台市和中国近代发展史上占有举足轻重的地位：清咸丰十一年（1861年）烟台开埠，20世纪初民族工商业建筑相继在老街上出现，20世纪30年代老街上形成了庞大的近代建筑物群。

Old Street on Yantai Hill

Located in Lixin Road, Zhifu District, the old street played a significant role in the history of modern China's development. In 1861, Yantai opened as a commercial port, and national industrial and commercial buildings have been in the old street since the early 20th century. In the 1930's, a large group of modern buildings were built in the old street.

烟台山朝阳街区

位于烟台市芝罘区烟台山下,是一片风格迥异的古建筑群。这里曾是17个国家的领事馆所在地,也是烟台近代制造业的发祥地,见证了烟台开埠150多年的历史。

Chaoyang Street on Yantai Hill

Located at the foot of Yantai Hill, it was the site of consulatesof seventeen countries as well as the birthplace of the modern manufacturing industry in Yantai. It has witnessed more than 150 years of historysince it was opened as a commercial port.

寒同山神仙洞

　　位于莱州城东南8000米处的寒同山山腰崖壁上，建于金元时期。传说开洞之时，忽然大雾遮山，貌不可辨，只闻凿锤之声，传至数里。40天后，雾散天晴，洞府、神像奇迹般地出现，故称"神仙洞"。

Fairy Cave of Hantong Hill

Located at the precipiceof Hantong Hill, which is 8,000 meters to Southeastern Laizhou City,it was built in the Jin(1115-1234) and Yuan(1206-1368)dynasties. According to legend, heavy fog suddenly covered the whole hill when the cave was completed. 40 days later, the fog dispersed and the weather was fine again and in all the caves there were miraculously statues of Buddha. The cave was called Fairy Cave after this.

长岛仙境阁

　　位于烟台市长岛县东部王沟村，建于1998年，是根据"海上仙山"的神话传说新建的景区，曾因出土一颗距今2.5万年的人类头骨化石和近百座墓葬而闻名。

Fairyland Pavilion of Long Island
Located in Wanggou Village, easternLong Island County, it was built in 1998 as a newly-built scenic area based on myths and legends of the fairy hill on the sea. It was famous for unearthing a 25,000 year - old fossil of a human skull and nearly one hundred tombs.

长岛九丈崖

位于烟台市长岛县长山岛的西北角,西依珍珠门水道,北邻国际航线长山水道。山崖险峻、水深流急、岩礁棋布,自然景观独树一帜。崖壁绵延400余米,尤以其崖壁罕见的石质组合和高峻险要而著名。

Jiuzhang Cliff
Located at thenorthwestern corner of ChangshanIsland, Long Island county, it stretches more than 400 meters,with Pearl Gate Waterway in the west and international Changshan Waterway in the north.It was especially famous for its rare combination of stones and steeps.

毓璜顶庙会

  又名"山会"，传说农历正月初九是玉皇大帝生日，这一天全国各地凡是供奉玉皇大帝神像的庙宇，都要赶庙会。此地庙会历史悠久、活动众多。

Yuhuangding Temple Fair

Also known as Mountain Fair, according to legend, January 9th in lunar calendar is the birthday of the Jade Emperor. All of the temples throughout the country who worship the statue of the Jade Emperor should have temple fairs on this day.

烟台面塑

烟台面塑以蓬莱、莱州、栖霞和招远等地为代表，面塑跟剪纸一样，讲求的是线条的柔美和纤细轻盈，面塑上的鸟雀之羽无论是描摹或剪下的都有风吹可动之感。

Yantai Dough Sculpture

The dough sculpture from Penglai, Laizhou, Qixia and Zhaoyuan are representatives of Yantai dough sculpting. Like paper cutting, dough sculpting also stresses the softness and lightness of the lines.

威海市
Weihai City

威海天后宫

位于威海属荣成市市区东北,建于清乾隆十六年(1751年),由山西洪洞县王一德建成。宫殿共分三进,为当时胶东一带较大的庙宇之一,据传当时进香朝拜者络绎不绝,曾盛极一时。

Temple of Queen of Heaven

Located at Northeastern Rongcheng City, it was built by Wang Yide from Hongtong County, Shanxi Province, in 1751. The grand, three-row temple buildings were popular in Jiadong at that time.

> 刘公庙

　　位于威海属刘公岛旅游码头东约300米处的丁公路北侧，传说在汉代，刘公、刘母曾多次拯救海上遇险的船民，后人为了纪念刘氏老人，在岛中部阳坡上建造了一座祠庙，在庙内塑造了刘公、刘母像。

LiugongTemple
Located at northern Dinggong Road, 300 meters to the east of a tourist dock in Liugong Island, it was built to commemorate Liu Gong and his wife during the Han Dynasty(202 B.C.-25 A.D.).

石岛赤山大佛

　　位于威海属荣成市石岛管理区,赤山自古是"佛"之胜地,站在经书石上东望,可见一座高约200米的山头,酷似一尊大佛,坐北朝南,正襟危坐。

Chishan Buddha of Stone Island

It is located in the Stone Island District, Rongcheng City. Standing on the inscription stone of Chishan Hill, you can see a 200-meter-high hill in the shape of Buddha. The south-facing Buddha sits seriously with a smaller figure of Buddha on both legs.

威海宽仁院

　　位于威海市环翠区海滨北路南段，建于清光绪二十八年（1902年），原为英商和记洋行露石台别墅，1934年作为抵债资产转移到天主教名下，由卢森堡黑衣修女将别墅扩充改建，在别墅以南修建了道院，即宽仁院。

Tolerance and Mercy Monastery
Located to the south of Haibin North Road, Huancui District, it was built by British merchants in 1902 and enlarged and rebuilt as a monastery by the nuns in black from Luxembourg in 1934. It was called Tolerance and Mercy Monastery.

> 海军提督署

　　位于威海市环翠区刘公岛上,建于清光绪十二年(1887年),为北洋海军的指挥机关,该建筑是威海的重要古迹。

Navy Praefect Bureau

Located in Liugong Island, Huancui District, it was built in 1887 as the command headquarters of the Beiyang Navy. It is an important historic site in Weihai.

水师学堂

　　位于威海市环翠区刘公岛西端，建于清光绪十五年（1889年），是清政府继福州船政学堂、天津水师学堂、广东水陆学堂之后创办的第四所培训海军军官的学堂。

NavalAcademy

Located at the west end of Liugong Island,Huancui District, it was built in 1889 as the fourth naval academy founded by the Qing government after FuzhouShippingAcademy, Tianjin Naval Academy and Guangdong Military and Naval Academy.

中国甲午战争博物馆陈列馆

　　位于威海市环翠区刘公岛，建于2005年，是一座全面展示中日甲午战争历史的综合性展馆。主体建筑由著名建筑设计师、中科院院士彭一刚教授设计，创造性地将象征北洋海军舰船的主体建筑与巍然矗立的北洋海军将领塑像融为一体。

The Museum of Sino-Japanese War of 1894-1895

Located in Liugong Island, Huancui District, it was built in 2005 as a comprehensive exhibition hall displaying the history of the Sino-Japanese war from 1894-1895. The major building was designed by Professor Peng Yigang, who is an academician of the Chinese Academy of Sciences and a famous architect.

小红楼

又称"将军楼",位于威海市环翠区西北山路北侧,建于1916年,两层欧式别墅建筑,原为英商私人住宅。

Little Red Tower

Also known as General Tower, located at the north of Xibeishan Road, Huancui District, it was built in 1916 as the private residence of British merchants. It is a two-storey Europeanstyle villa.

威海四眼楼

位于威海市环翠区环海路七号，始建于清光绪二十四年（1898年），原为英租威海卫时期英国海军司令的别墅，是目前威海保留的比较完整的古建筑文物之一。其建筑外观上传承了英国文艺复兴时期风格，因主体建筑前上方有四个石制圆孔，故称"四眼楼"。

Four Eyes Building
Located at No. 7, Huanhai Road, Huancui District, it was built in 1898 as the residence of the commander of the British navy and is a well-preserved historic architectural relic. It was named after the four round stone holes on the main building.

> 海草房

　　主要位于胶东半岛的威海、烟台、青岛等沿海地带，特别是荣成地区更为集中。据考证，海草房从秦汉至宋金逐步形成并在胶东半岛广为流传，到了元明清则进入繁荣时期。海草房可以说是世界上最具有代表性的生态民居之一。

Seaweed House

It is mainly located in the coastal areas like Weihai, Yantai and Qingdao of the Jiaodong Peninsula, especially in Rongcheng. The seaweed house is one of the most representative ecological residences in the world.

| 六角楼 |

　　位于威海市环翠区东山路，建于清光绪二十八年（1902年），最初是供旅华欧洲人避暑时租用的建筑，现在因年久失修已成为了危房。

Hexagonal Tower
Located in Dongshan Road,Huancui District, it was built in 1902 as a rentable house in the summer for Europeans living in China. After long years of being out of repair, it is now a dilapidated building .

华勇营旧址

　　位于威海市北山路西侧，建于清光绪二十八年（1902年），欧式二层楼建筑，木石结构，铁瓦坡屋顶，东部为四层钟楼，为英国殖民当局在威海招募中国人组成的华勇营旧址。

Chinese RegimentSite
Located at the west of Beishan Road, it was built in 1902 as a European style two-storey building. It was the site of the Chinese regiment, which was aChinese army recruited by British colonial authorities in Weihai.

威海老洋房

位于威海市区和刘公岛上，多数都建于19世纪末英国强租威海卫后，建筑风格鲜明，现已成为城市历史文化遗产的一部分。

Old Western StyleHouses in Weihai

Located in Liugong Island,Weihai City, it was built at the end of the 19th century after Britainoccupied Weihai. It ispart of the city's historical and cultural heritage with its distinctive architectural style.

> 威海卫

　　位于山东半岛东北端，濒临黄海、西连烟台、北隔渤海海峡与辽东半岛旅顺口势成犄角，共为渤海锁钥，拱卫京津海上门户。威海卫原为滨海渔村，汉称石落。

Weihai Port

Located in Weihai City, the northeast of Shandong Peninsula, it is close to the Yellow Sea and next to Yantai in the west, while forming a corner together with Lvshun Port of Liaodong Peninsula in the north, thus becoming the ocean gateways to Beijing and Tianjin.

威海炮台

　　位于威海海岸山坡及山顶，始建于清光绪五年（1879年），后炮台在水师学堂堞墙北150米之小山上，包括地下掩蔽与炮位两部分。掩蔽建于山阳坡，辟有南北向坑道，东西成一排，开七个门洞，坑道内壁以方石料两面起券坡覆。地面炮位两座，均呈圆坑形，直径13.4米。

Weihai Forts

Located on top of a hillside in the coastal area of Weihai, it was built in 1879. The back fort was located on the hill 150 meters to the northern wall of the Naval Academy. The shelter was built on the southern slope and two round pit- shaped emplacements with diameters of 13.4 meters each were set on the ground.

威海定远舰

　　位于威海市环翠区。定远舰是清政府花费近170万两白银向德国订造的一艘战舰，该舰装甲厚、吨位大、炮火重，利于防御，号称"第一铁舰"，是当时世界海军中罕见的大型铁甲舰。清光绪二十一年（1895年）被炸毁，现有战舰为依据历史资料按1：1比例复制的复制品。

Dingyuan Warship of Weihai
The Dingyuan warship was ordered by Qing government to Germany and built by the Vulkan shipyard of Germany. It was launched on November 28, 1883 as one of the largest navy ironclads in the world.

| 幸福门 |

　　位于威海港南侧100米处，建于2005年，被誉为"威海之门"，是威海的标志，代表着威海现代化的城市形象。

Well BeingGate
Located at 100 meters to the south of Weihai Port, it was built in 2005 and known as the Gate of Weihai. It is the symbol of Weihai.

> 悦海灯塔

　　位于威海市环翠区滨海大道悦海公园主广场中心区，是提供给游人远观瞭望及休闲聚会的场所，灯塔主题意义为"归航"。

Yuehai Lighthouse
Located in the centre of the main square of Yuehai Park, Binhai Avenue, Huancui District, it is a venue for tourists to look out, relax and gather.The theme of the lighthouse is Home.

刘公岛皂埠嘴炮台

　　位于威海湾南岸，现为南帮炮台遗址，始建于清光绪十三年（1887年），共五座炮台，海岸炮台即皂埠嘴炮台，有火炮六门。

Zaobuzhui Fort in Liugong in Island

Located on the south bank of Weihai Harbour, built in 1887, it is the site of Nanbang Fort. There are fiveforts andHaian Fort was the original Zaobuzhui Fort and had six guns.

| 日岛炮台 |

　　位于刘公岛东南2000米的海面上，建于清光绪年间（1875～1908年），因从陆上清晨远眺，日岛恰处东方日出方位，又因它是威海海湾最早见到日出的地方，故得名"日岛"。日岛炮台在甲午威海卫港保卫战中发挥了重要的作用。

Sun Island Fort

Located on the sea,which is 2,000 meters to Southeastern Liugong Island, it was built from1875 to 1908. When you overlook the sea, the Sun Island is located in the direction of the sunrise. It's also the eastern end of Weiai harbor, and embraces first sunrise. This is why it was named Sun Island.

{ 海驴岛灯塔 }

　　位于荣城市西霞口村，始建于1953年，原为灯桩，为灰色铁架结构，1976年改建为七米高的白色圆柱形石塔。现在的海驴岛灯塔建于1990年，白色六边形砖混结构，外贴马赛克。

Lighthouse of Hailu Island

Located in Hailu Island, north of eastern Shandong Peninsula, it was built in 1953 as a light beacon and rebuilt into a white, cylindrical stone tower afterwards. It is a white, hexagonal brick concrete structure lighthouse now.

成山头

又称"成山角"或"天尽头",位于荣成市成山镇,因地处成山山脉最东端而得名。成山头三面环海,一面接陆,与韩国隔海相望,仅距94海里,是最早看见海上日出的地方,自古就被誉为"太阳升起的地方"。

Cheng Hilltop

Also known as Cheng Hill Corner or "The End of the Earth," it is located in the Chengshan Town of Rongcheng City. It was named after the location of the eastern end of the Chengshan Mountain range and you can see the first sunrise over the sea from there.

成山头灯塔

位于荣城市成山头岬角，始建于清嘉庆二十五年（1821年），战争期间遭到破坏，1950年重修。主要作用是为航经成山头水域的船舶提供助航服务，灯塔附近设有成山头船舶交通管理中心（VTS）和雷达站。

Lighthouse on Cheng Hilltop

Located at the cape of Cheng Hilltop, east end of Shandong Peninsula, it was built in 1821 and rebuilt in 1950 after being destroyed during the war. The main function of this lighthouse is to provide navigational aid to the ships passing through the water around Cheng Hilltop.

圣经山

位于威海市文登区葛家镇西北区，方圆近八平方千米，是"海上仙山之祖"的胶东半岛第一山——昆嵛山南延的支脉。

Bible Hill

Located in the northwest of Gejia Town, Wendeng District, it covers an area of 8,000 square meters. It is the branch of the South Kunlun Mountain range, which is the first mountain in the Jiaodong peninsula.

胶东大鼓

　　起源于盲人调，流行于山东胶东半岛沿海一线，过去多以艺人所在县命名。民间艺人梁前光在抗日战争胜利前后，曾在胶东一带及济南旅大、蚌埠以及河南邵县等地随军演唱新编的曲词，被称为梁派大鼓，1949年定名为胶东大鼓。

Jiaodong Bass Drum
Originatingfrom the melody of blind performers, it is popular in the Jiaodong Peninsula and coastal area nearby. It was formerly named for the county from which the performer came and eventually titled Jiaodong Bass Drum in 1949.

祭祀渔神

　　渔民首次出海拉网，当捕到鱼之后，首先要捡大鱼蒸熟盛于盘中，在船头奠酒焚香，祈祷龙王爷保佑海上发财。几条船在一起捕鱼时，谁的船先打上鱼来，谁就放炮敲锣，并拣最大的鱼供在船头。

To Worship the God ofFishing
When fishermen caught fish during their first trip of the year, they would pick up the biggest fish firstand steam it before dishing it out. They would also pour sacrificial wine andburnincense to pray to the Dragon Lord for blessings and fortune.

新船点睛

渔船是渔民赖以为生的依靠,渔民对它爱护备至,并赋予灵性。过去每条渔船都做一对凸起的大眼睛,新船造好后只画眼不画睛,等到黄道吉日,船主会敲锣打鼓亲自为新船点睛,其他的渔民也会喊着大吉大利的号子,把披红挂绿的新船一步一步从岸上移下海去。

Putting in the Pupils on a New Boat
Fishermen take good care of their fishing boats as they are living tools for them. In the past, every new fishing boatwas finished with two big protruding eyes without pupils. The owner of the fishing boat will put in the pupils on the auspicious day by himself.

荣成国际渔民节

每三年举办一次，以渔村文化为主要内容，开展各种海上运动、大型民俗观光旅游活动、经济技术贸易洽谈和海洋渔业博览会等活动。

Rongcheng International Fishermen Festival
It is held every three years and focuses on the culture of the fishing village. During the festival, many kinds of water sports and big folk tourism events will be organized.

> 乳山大秧歌

　　乳山大秧歌是一种具有浓郁的地方特色的汉族民间舞蹈,与海阳大秧歌同宗同族,均负盛名。海阳大秧歌、胶州大秧歌、商河鼓子秧歌,并称山东三大秧歌。

Rushan Dayangge
It is a kind of Han nationality folk dancing with rich local characteristics. It is part of the same clan and race as Haiyang Dayangge. Both enjoy a great reputation.

乳山夏西火龙秧歌

　　乳山夏西火龙秧歌具有浓郁的地方特色。秧歌闹起来的时候，遥看恢宏豪放，近看节律紧凑。秧歌起源，民间有"周朝秧歌唐朝戏"的说法。

Rushan Xiaxi Huolong Yangge
It has richlocal characteristics and the performance looks vigorous, magnificent from afar whilethe rhythmic sounds feel like they get closer and closer.

祭海神

　　人们提前购好供品，杀猪，去毛烙皮，涂上朱红色的颜料，由男人抬着到龙王庙或海边，摆好供品，敲锣打鼓、鞭炮齐鸣，面海跪祭、供奉"海神"。

To Worship the God of Sea

People purchase offerings in advance-killing the pigs, removing the hair, burning the skin and coating it with red pigment before they were carried by men to the Dragon King Temple or the beach. After that, people place offerings properly, beat drums, and go down on their knees while facing the sea to worship the God of the Sea.

日照市
Rizhao City

护国万寿光明寺（一）

位于日照市五莲山风景区，始建于唐代，中兴于明代。依山而建，曲径通幽，奇峰异石众星捧月地环立在寺周围，梵宇山光交相辉映，置身其中顿生超尘之感。

The Brightness Temple of Longevity (1)
Located in the Five Lotus Mountain scenic area, it was built in the Tang Dynasty(618-907) and thrived in the Ming Dynasty(1368-1644).Built beside the mountain with winding paths leading to a secluded spot, it is surrounded by picturesque peaks and rocks and the temple and mountain enhance each other's beauty. You will feel detached from the world when you place yourself in the temple.

护国万寿光明寺（二）

　　山东有四大禅寺：长清灵岸寺、益都法庆寺、诸城侔云寺和日照光明寺。光明寺是一座由皇帝敕赐寺名，内库拨款，太监亲临监工的御建寺院。

The Brightness Temple of Longevity (2)

The Brightness Templewas a royal temple named by the Emperor, financed by the royal court and supervised by eunuchs during the construction. It is one of the four biggest temples in Shandong.

五莲山景区

位于日照市五莲山县东南,因五莲列峤、耸接云霄、如莲花初放而得名,总面积68平方千米,由五莲山、九仙山两大风景区组成。景区内自然景观和人文景观众多,以奇、秀、险、怪、幽、旷、奥七大特色著称。

Five LotusMountain Scenic Area

Located in southeastern WulianshanCounty, it was named after the shape of mountains which looked like five lotus flowers. It covers a total area of 68 square kilometers and consists of Five Lotus Mountain and Nine Immortals Mountain.

五莲山

　　五莲山全山28峰，主峰五莲峰海拔515.7米，奇峰怪石、秀丽多姿，北宋大文学家苏东坡曾赞该山"奇秀不减雁荡"。

Five Lotus Mountain

There are 28 peaks in Five Lotus Mountain and the main peak, Five Lotus peak, is 515.7 meters above sea level. The great litterateur Su Dongpo of the Northern Song Dynasty(960-1127)was impressed by the great variety of peaks and stones here and praised the Five Lotus Mountain for being as beautiful as Yandang Mountain in Wenzhou, Zhejiang.

日照市街景（一）

　　日照因日光先照而得名，素有"东方太阳城"之美誉。沿海从南到北60千米的金沙滩，被誉为"中国沿海未被污染的黄金海岸"，日照最主要的景点都集中于此。

Street View of Rizhao City (1)

Rizhao means sunlight and the city got its name from the sunlight here. The 60-kilometer-long golden beach from the south to the north enjoys the fame of being an uncontaminated golden beach i.

日照市街景（二）

日照旅游资源丰富，海、山、古、林兼备，境内有金沙滩、奥林匹克水上运动公园、五莲山风景区、莒县浮来山风景区等景区。

Street View of Rizhao City (2)

Rizhao City boasts rich tourism resources, including Golden Beach, the Olympic Water Sports Park, Five Lotus Mountain Scenic Area and Fulai Mountain Scenic Area of Lu County, etc.

| 日照火车站 |

　　全称"济南铁路局日照站",原名"石臼所站",位于日照市东港区海滨五路1号,1986年1月1日正式成立并开通运营,1994年4月更名为日照站。

Rizhao Railway Station
Originally known as Shijiusuo Station, its full name is Rizhao Station of Jinan Railway Bureau.It is located at No. 1, Haibin Five Road, Donggang District and was opened to traffic in 1986.

日照港

位于日照市东港区上海路，建于1982年，1986年投产运营，是我国重点发展的沿海20个主枢纽港之一，是伴随着我国改革开放诞生、成长起来的新兴沿海港口。

Rizhao Port

Located in Shanghai Road, Donggang District, it was built in 1982 and went into operation in 1986. It was one of the twenty main hub ports developed by the government alongthe coast in China.

> 日照灯塔

　　原名"石臼灯塔",建于1985年,1992年更名,是日照海滨港口城市的象征。高36.2米,灯光射程18海里,主要功能是为日照近海及进出日照港的船舶提供导航服务。

Rizhao Lighthouse
Formerly known as Shijiu Lighthouse, it was built in 1985 and renamed Rizhao Lighthouse in 1992. It is the symbol of Rizhao City.

万平口风景区

　　位于日照市东港区，是南来北往的商船停泊之地，有江北最大的天然泻湖，是天然的避风港，每年都会有万艘船只从南方运大米到北方来。

WanpingkouScenic Area

Located in Donggang District, it is a berth of commercial ships from different places as well as a natural haven. Every year thousands of ships carry rice from the south to the north.

日照帆船基地

　　位于日照市万平口自然泻湖始端，总面积106公顷，可停泊320艘帆船、80艘游艇，可以承办国际奥运所有水上项目各个级别的帆船比赛，是2008年北京奥运会水上项目的赛前训练基地。

Sailing Boat Base of Rizhao

Located at the starting end of a natural lagoon in Wanpingkou, covering a total area of 106 hectares, it can offer berths to 320 sailing boats and 80 yachts. Itwas the training base for water sports during the 2008 Beijing Olympic Games.

龙王节

又称"渔民节",是日照沿海渔民在长期生产生活中形成的一种传统习俗。传说农历六月十三是海龙王的生日,这天要举行敬龙王仪式,祈求一年出海平安、鱼虾满舱。

The Dragon King Festival

Also known as Fishermen Festival. According to legend, June 13 in the Lunar calendar is the birthday of the Dragon King and the ceremony of worshiping the Dragon King should be held on this day to pray for safety and good fortune in fishing

渔民节（一）

渔民节中渔民们准备了各式贡品祭海，祈求人福舟安、渔业丰收。跑旱船又称荡湖船、划水船，女子双手持竹木制作的船形道具，艄公持橹在旁做划船状，边行边舞。辅之以伴奏，表演诙谐。

Fishermen Festival (1)

Fishermen prepared various offerings to worship the sea during the festival to pray for safety and the fishing harvest.Land Boat Dancing is performed by women holding bamboo boat props in their hands while helmsman row with sculls. They dance while walking.

渔民节（二）

　　渔民们带着宰杀过的生猪和供品，随着鞭炮，在彩旗和秧歌队的簇拥下，来到一处渔船停靠码头。主事宣布祭拜活动开始，渔民们摆上供品，倒上美酒，点燃供香，面朝大海进行祭拜。渔民节已被列入国家级非物质文化遗产保护名录。

Fishermen Festival (2)
After the chief announced the beginning of worship, fishermen placed offerings properly before pouring the wine, lighting incense and facing the seato worship. The Fishermen Festival is on the list of "National Non-Material Cultural Heritage".